FLOWERS OF FLAME

FLOWERS OF FLAME

UNHEARD VOICES OF IRAQ

EDITED BY

Sadek Mohammed
Soheil Najm
Haider Al-Kabi
Dan Veach

MICHIGAN STATE UNIVERSITY PRESS ▪ *East Lansing*

♾ The paper used in this publication meets the minimum requirements of ANSI/NISO Z39.48-1992 (R 1997) (Permanence of Paper).

 Michigan State University Press
East Lansing, Michigan 48823-5245

Printed and bound in the United States of America.

14 13 12 11 10 09 08   1 2 3 4 5 6 7 8 9 10

LIBRARY OF CONGRESS CATALOGING-IN-PUBLICATION DATA
Flowers of flame: unheard voices of Iraq / edited by Sadek Mohammed . . .
[et al.].
p. cm.
Includes bibliographical references.
ISBN 978-0-87013-842-3 (pbk. : alk. paper) 1. Arabic poetry—Iraq—
Translations into English. I. Mohammed, Sadek, 1964–
PJ8044.5.E5F46 2008
892.7'170809567—dc22
    2008029432

Some of these poems first appeared in the special IRAQ Issue of ATLANTA REVIEW

Cover design by Erin Kirk New
Book design by Sharp Des!gns, Inc., Lansing, Michigan
Cover art ©iStockphoto.com/Ben Heys. Used with permission.

g green press INITIATIVE Michigan State University Press is a member of the Green Press Initiative and is committed to developing and encouraging ecologically responsible publishing practices. For more information about the Green Press Initiative and the use of recycled paper in book publishing, please visit *www.greenpressinitiative.org.*

Visit Michigan State University Press on the World Wide Web at
www.msupress.msu.edu

Contents

WELCOME

Dan Veach

Despite years of war and tsunamis of sound bites, this will be the first opportunity many readers will have to meet Iraqis as real human beings, speaking heart to heart. In these pages you will hear the unheard voices of Iraq: men and women, Sunnis, Shias, and Kurds.

These poems were collected, as the war raged all around them, by Iraqis living and working in Baghdad. This is their message to the world, one that transcends all the barriers dividing present-day Iraq. It is a message that needs to be heard by all sides in the current conflict.

Iraq's poets have suffered imprisonment, exile, and death for the truths they have dared to tell. Poetry is not a luxury in Iraq, but a vital part of the struggle for the nation's future. This is poetry that is feared by tyrants and would-be tyrants.

How do they do it? How is it even possible to write poetry in present-day Iraq? One poet asks himself, "How can you extract poems and shrapnel from your chest at the very same time?" The answers that you'll find here will amaze you—a "perfect storm" of international headline news, profound humanity, and genuinely great art.

You'll find joy here as well as struggle. Arabic poetry has a long and rich tradition of ecstatic love, whimsical humor, and philosophic insight. Remarkably, charm and lightness of touch abound. Even the war invites you to a picnic—from which you will not return untouched.

These poems form a continuous "conversation," each one speaking to and illuminating those around it. The subjects taken up in turn are war, love, the daily life of the people, and the inner life of the artist. An Iraqi emergency room physician in Baghdad, someone who has surely seen the worst of the current conflict, recently read this collection in English. When he told us that these poems had brought him to tears, I knew that we had captured at least a little of the truth about Iraq.

Many of these poems were written in response to the American invasion of Iraq in 2003. "Tomorrow the War Will Have a Picnic," for instance, was composed on the eve of the "shock and awe" campaign against Baghdad. We see here, through Iraqi eyes, the fall of Saddam's statue, his trial, the ongoing sectarian violence, and the foreign invaders on both sides of the struggle.

Others reflect the fact that Iraq has been at war for a long, long time. Almost immediately after taking power, Saddam plunged Iraq into a war with Iran that lasted from 1980 to 1988 and cost, by some estimates, a million lives between the two sides. Nothing was gained, and the economies of both countries were ruined by the conflict.

Iraq's desperate financial situation after the war figured largely in Saddam's decision to invade oil-rich Kuwait, which led to the 1991 Gulf War with the United States. Before and during the war, the United States encouraged the Iraqi people—by means of radio broadcasts, air-dropped leaflets and public speeches by President Bush—to overthrow Saddam Hussein. Hopeful of American support, the Iraqi people did rise up against Saddam at the war's end, and actually succeeded in taking over most of the provinces of Iraq.

However, America stood by as Saddam crushed the poorly armed rebellion. American troops were instructed not to aid the rebels in any way, and Saddam's attack helicopters were allowed to fly freely in the "no fly" zones. The result was a terrible slaughter: more than a hundred thousand Shiites and Kurds were killed and buried in mass graves such as the one described in "Bags of Bones."

Saddam, himself a Sunni Arab, had a long history of torturing and persecuting Iraq's majority Shiite population and its Kurdish ethnic minority. Many of the poets in this book have been driven into exile. Others were killed or "disappeared" during his regime. For them, and for those who lie buried in mass graves across Iraq, these poems remain as a lasting monument.

The View from Baghdad

Sadek Mohammed

Soheil Najm and I started work on an anthology of Iraqi poetry in the summer of 2005, immediately after my return from a self-imposed exile in various countries. Everything was different in the country and in our city, Baghdad. Life was absolutely impossible. There was no electricity, no fuel, and no potable water. Even if we wanted to meet, we had to take our chances through car bombs, roadside bombs, mortar shelling, and the death squads that were massacring the city. A translator was, indeed, perceived as a traitor in that hellish atmosphere, and many were assassinated under the pretext of being collaborators with the "occupation forces."

There were many moments in which I wanted to abandon this work. It was Soheil's inexhaustible patience and solid belief in the importance of what we were doing that kept me going on. But above all I was getting a real therapeutic effect from the poetry itself, especially that of the poets who had remained in Iraq and who, in spite of the suffocating atmosphere, were able to express creatively the permanent concerns of the Iraqi soul and its yearning for beauty, freedom, justice, and peace.

We have three generations of poets here, according to the traditional classification of poets in Iraq. A generation is conceived, according to this classification, as a group of poets who started to write and first became known in a certain decade. In reality, all of the poets in this anthology can be classified as one generation. Historically, they all belong to the same era. Artistically, they all use the free verse form of modern Iraqi poetry, which was primarily initiated in Arab poetry by Nazik Al-Malaeka, Badr Shakir Al-Sayyab, Abdul Wahab Al-Bayati, and Buland Al-Haidari. Thematically, the majority of them deal with injustice, war, isolation, alienation, exile, poverty, the will to live in the face of the death forces, and the yearning for beauty. One can safely say that all of their poetry is an outcry against the forces that were depriving the Iraqi soul of its basic rights.

Since the 1970s, only a small, fortunate group of Iraqi poets have been translated. The majority have been marginalized or neglected. They were writing in very difficult times: every word was scrutinized by a brutal, ignorant censorship. "You are either with us or against us" was the motto of the merciless guardians of the literary establishment. "With us," according to the logic of the authorities, meant chanting hymns in praise of the dominant ideology and the futile wars of its leaders. "Against us" meant any suspicion of free, independent thinking, whether or not it threatened their ideology or their leader.

It was a difficult period that witnessed the migration or, indeed, the exile of the best of the best of the Iraqi talents. Thus, two categories came into being: "residing poetry" and "exile poetry." Those who continued to live in Iraq rarely knew about what was written in exile and vice versa. They took separate paths in their evolution and enrichment, until they became two separate entities. But both remained attached to the land of their birth.

This created the problem of locating "exile poetry" from Iraqi poets who had migrated to every corner of the world. Furthermore, not all "residing" poets enjoyed the luxury of getting their poetry formally published. Many of them were personally typing and photocopying their collections, which were privately circulated among a narrow circle of friends and acquaintances.

The fear of not finding adequate literary material from this period was a valid one. But when I carried my idea of translating contemporary Iraqi poetry to my friend, the renowned poet and translator Soheil Najm, he put in my hands a treasure of sources that he had been meticulously collecting and archiving through the years. He also contacted scores of Iraqi poets, in Iraq and all over the world, and asked them to send their poetry. Had it not been for him, a timid introvert like me would not have been able to contribute anything to a work such as this. And so we agreed to prepare and translate this anthology together.

A Note on Arabic Verse

Modern Iraqi poets in the late 1940s felt that the meters of traditional Arabic poetry were too rigid to be followed. There are fifteen different meters of rhymed traditional Arabic poetry. A meter is called a *bahr,* which translates literally as "sea" in English. A "sea" is based on a complex system of systematically alternating longer and shorter syllables. In addition to this there is the rhyme scheme, which is determined by the last consonant sound of a word. Normally, a single rhyme is used, even in poems of 100 lines or more.

Traditional poems employ one meter and one rhyme scheme, and both are followed rigorously throughout the poem. Some poets felt that following the metrics of traditional Arabic poetry was a hindrance to their ability to express themselves freely. So they devised a new style of writing which allowed the use of a variety of traditional meters within one poem, as well as greater freedom in the rhyme scheme. They called this new way of writing *shi'ir hur,* which translates as "free poetry." This was a literary revolution that radically changed the entire Arab literary scene and marked the beginning of modernist Arabic literature.

The impetus for this development came from many sources. It arose at a time of revolutions and liberation from the colonial powers, mainly the Ottomans and the British. This history inspired its literary equivalent in the form of a revolt against the classical ways and the liberation of poets from the rigidities of tradition. Socio-culturally, the traditional ways of writing poetry were seen as unsuited to the new forms of social life and the great strides being made on the road of modernization. Educationally, a high level of literacy enabled many writers to get acquainted with world literature and its major figures, sometimes in translation and sometimes in the mother tongue. The four pioneer Iraqi poets who initiated this break with tradition were influenced by T. S. Eliot and Edith Sitwell.

This innovative evolution was taken a step further by Arab poets in other countries (primarily Syria and Lebanon), who entirely did away with the traditional metrics of Arabic poetry. The influence of Arthur Rimbaud and the French Symbolists was a major factor in this development. The resulting "prose poetry" was seen as the final frontier of expression for modernist Arabic poetry. Many Iraqi poets followed suit, regarding prose poetry as the natural outcome of the modernist trend that had been initiated by their Iraqi brethren. The resulting clash between traditionalist and modernist Arab poetry is still being felt even to this day.

A Poetry Workshop Named Iraq

Haider Al-Kabi

Early in July 2006, Soheil Najm, Iraqi poet and translator, sent me from Baghdad the English translation of an anthology of Iraqi poetry from 1970 to the present, compiled and translated by himself and Dr. Sadek Mohammed. Though then unfinished, the anthology presented a sweeping, panoramic, and fresh view of the poetry of present-day Iraq. It vividly reflected the grim atmosphere that envelops the country today, the stark and harsh reality of the predicament of the Iraqi people, their worries and fears and hopes and dreams and, above all, their resolve to triumph over the nightmarish circumstances surrounding them.

For my part, I was working on translating poems by some of my departed friends, such as Adam Hatem, Mahmud Al-Braikan, and Abd Al-Hassan Al-Shathr, friends whom I always admired for the indestructible and rebellious spirit manifested in their poetry and in their personalities. Paying homage to our lifelong friendship, I started with Adam Hatem, who had led a life overwhelmed with misery and suffering, running away from political oppression in his homeland, only to die in Lebanon, weighed down with poverty, hunger, and homelessness. When I sent my translation of his poem "That Is My Life" and one of Soheil's poems to *Atlanta Review*, it never occurred to me that I would find myself all of a sudden involved in a larger project, one in which the whole spectrum of more than three decades of Iraqi poetry would be represented.

In his response, Dan Veach, *Atlanta Review*'s editor, asked me if I was able to participate in the making of a special issue dedicated to Iraqi poetry. Readily I answered in the affirmative, thanks to Soheil and Sadek, who had entrusted their work to me. So I added my translations to theirs and sent the whole collection to Dan, for him to choose from.

My communication with my friends in Iraq was not all that easy. Apart from the costliness of phone calls to Iraq, my friends' telephones were frequently dead, and access to their email boxes was repeatedly blocked. At times, it took me more than a month to get an answer to an email, and some never seem to have reached them at all. Regular mail, however, was much more frustrating. Now if that was the case with poets who were known to us, what about those others, inside and outside Iraq, of whose contact information we knew nothing?

Technicalities aside, there is something very important for the reader to bear in mind. In a society torn among political factions like modern Iraq, it would be unthinkable, from the government's point of view, for an Iraqi artist, especially a poet, not to have an allegiance to some political entity or other. "Allegiance" was expressed either by membership in a political party or through the sentiments reflected in the poet's writing. Accordingly, poets were classified either as proponents or opponents of the system. Notwithstanding their artistic merits, poets opposing the regime were deliberately overlooked; those supporting it were brought to the fore. During the thirty-odd years in which the Baath Party and Saddam Hussein's Baathist regime ruled the country, many poets, some of whom were endowed with considerable talents, were transformed either by temptation or intimidation into mere propagandists.

On the other hand, some of the most distinguished poets, such as Mohammad Mahdi Al-Jawahiri, Buland Al-Haidari, Lamee'a Abbas Amara, Saadi Youssef, Fadhil Al-Azzawi, and Muzaffar Al-Nawwab, fled the country. Most of the aforementioned poets had experienced imprisonment; some, for instance Buland Al-Haidari, were under death sentence and were released only because of their reputation as poets. Others, such as Mahmud Al-Braikan, the only poet from earlier generations represented in this selection, had distanced themselves from the literary scene and resorted to silence. But whereas notable poets had been spared the worst, younger poets were more susceptible to government oppression. Being unknown, their disappearance would pass unnoticed. Thus many younger Iraqi poets also went into exile. Against such a background of agitation, division, and conflict, a mixed feeling of bitterness, distrust, and at times hostility existed among poets of different political stances.

As a result, the making of a comprehensive poetry anthology in today's Iraq is a truly intimidating task. First of all, one must overcome one's own feelings toward those poets whose political stand opposes one's own. Next, one has to have access to poets scattered all over the planet. Then, one needs to convince those poets to participate.

Besides all this, one must consider the multiplicity of languages in which Iraqi poets write: some in Arabic, some in Kurdish, some in Turkoman. Poems originally written in languages other than Arabic had to be rendered into Arabic first. Then comes the translation of the selected poems into English. Only those few who have tackled literary translation from Arabic into English can describe the agony, pain, and frustration associated with such an undertaking. It is truly impressive that such an achievement was accomplished by two individuals working alone amidst the circumstances described above, equipped only with their determination to bring to the world an authentic and up-to-date picture of that huge poetry workshop named Iraq.

A PRESENT

Come.
You won't regret it.
It is a small miracle
that God granted me.
Come.
A green
rose.
A bottle
whose perfume
is never drained,
that encircles you like a halo.
There,
you'll see it, you'll smell it, you'll hear it.
It is a poem hanging
from
its hair
like a chandelier in my grave.
Take it.

JAMAL MUSTAFA
translated by Haider Al-Kabi

THE HEART OF A WOMAN

The heart of a woman is the only country
That I can enter without a passport,
Where no policeman
Asks me for my card
Or searches my suitcase
Full of contraband joys
Forbidden poems
And delicious sorrows.
The heart of a woman is the only country
That does not heap up heavy weapons
Nor force its citizens to fight its wars.

Lateef Helmet

translated by Soheil Najm

THE PREY

Like a flock of eagles on their wounded prey
The furies have descended on Iraq
In spite of all their hatred for each other.
Each night they return to their lairs
Under the wing of darkness,
Oblivious to the blood
That smears their mouths.
But shame will seize their souls
When they discover, in the morning light
The prey they feasted on last night
Was the flesh of their own children.

ADIL ABDULLAH
translated by Soheil Najm

NIGHT PRAYERS

from *Slightly Quarrelsome Texts*

You see your God only
In blades and blood.
I see Him
In a word,
In a song,
In the deep blue of her eyes,
And in the sea. . . .

You, whose life passes by so fast
Spend all your time
Disputing of God and Satan,
And can't spare a single moment
To understand
The heart of your fellow man. . . .

My God
Is One.
He is neither a Catholic,
Nor a Protestant,
Neither a Sunni
Nor a Shia'a.
Those who divide Him up,
Who interpret Him,
Who fabricate His sayings,
Who classify Him
According to their faiths,
Their demands,
Their constitutions
And their armies—
They are the ones who deny
The truth of God.

ADNAN AL-SAYEGH
translated by Soheil Najm

BAGS OF BONES

What luck!
At last she has found his bones.
His skull is also in the bag.
The bag in her hand
Is just like all the other bags
In other shivering hands.
His bones look like thousands of bones
In the mass graveyard.
But his skull is unlike
Any other skull.
Two eyes, two holes—
He saw too much through them.
Two holes for ears
To let the music in.
The story of this skull
Is his alone.
A nose
That is just an empty gap,
A mouth open
Like an abyss—
It was not like this
When he kissed her
There, quietly
Far from this place
With its clatter of skulls, bones, and dust.
This place where all our questions are exhumed:
What does it mean to die all this death
In a place where darkness plays
The instrument of silence?
What does it mean to meet
Your loved ones now
With all these holes?

To give your mother back,
On the occasion of death,
The handful of bones
She offered you
On the occasion of birth?
What does it mean that you depart
Without a death certificate?
The dictator does not give a receipt
When he takes your life.
The dictator must have a heart,
Perhaps a balloon that never bursts.
And a skull too: a huge one,
Unlike any other.
His skull, alone, has figured all this out—
How to multiply one death by millions
To equal the country.
He is the director of this tragedy,
And as his audience applauds
It shakes the bones,
The bones in the bags,
The full bag in her hand at last.
Her luck, at least a little better
Than her neighbor, who, alas
Still goes on looking
For her bag
Of bones.

DUNYA MIKHAIL
translated by Sadek Mohammed

BOMBARDMENT

The city sits quietly
The sky, above her, is
A hammer

The city is empty
Whispers disturb her tranquility
Steps glitter
And their echoes
Like bats
Cling to balconies

The city is jammed with vehicles
Vainly
They spin their wheels
On the oil
Of the streets

The city breaks her mirror—
The river
Splitting her
Like a crooked slash

The river rises upward in a blaze
Seagulls stretch out their necks
Amid the shipwrecks—
The river collapses
And drags them to the bottom

The city cannot
Gather in her children.
Sometimes they crawl
Sometimes they fly

They cling to her like sins
They are flung like fruits
Her branches vainly reaching out for them
She tries to break loose from her roots
To gather up her little ones
The city is standing
Her head in her hands
She swirls
Swirls
Swirls
Becomes dizzy
Sinks amid signboards

The city takes a cup
Of water
To swallow her words

Now she is hushed
Silencing her children
Straining her ears
She waits the sudden falling
Of the sky

HAIDER AL-KABI

translated by Sadek Mohammed

THE STATUE

Fearsome
In the night of the square
The statue was
Filled with power.
Fire
Shot forth from its cement forehead.
Among the people
Rumors were spread:
"A holy man."
"He heals the leprous
And the blind."
"He resurrects the dead
From their sleep."
We saw it in its Sufi stance
Lifting a white hand skyward
To clasp the polar star,
Squeeze out its light
And collect the blazing sparks
In baskets.
Among the people
Rumors were spread:
"We saw him speaking with an infant in its cradle.
And when he touches the mountains,
Solid rocks,
By his might,
Become gold
And pearls."
Among the people
Rumors were spread:
"If he wishes,
He can make the sun rise from the west."
And the Magi of the time agreed:

"He came
To save us
From the thirst of fire
And from wearing rags."
The Communists said:
"We saw him
Wearing his spectacles
To add luminous lines
To *Das Kapital*."
Among the people
Rumors were spread:
The Imam of the mosque,
Weaving his story, said:
"He came to us from the other world
Carrying his green paradise
For the poor,
And he came as hell for the wicked."
A woman in her wedding gown was seen
Slipping off her chastity near the pedestal, saying:
"Extinguish my heart's ember,
Devastate me completely,
Break the rust of my locks."
Among the people
Rumors were spread.

But the seer, the visionary,
Said in secret to the waves:
"I see a flood
Of the wind's blood surging.
I see necks hanging
From a boot strap."

And when the firestorm blew
In the center of the square
The solid rock pedestal
Tilted, swayed, and
The statue fell
From the heights of its myth.
Rocks shattered, scattered
Were carried by the tail
Of the wind's black cloak
To the dustbin.

ABDUL RAZAQ AL-RUBAIEE
translated by Sadek Mohammed

SEVEN ATTEMPTS TO PORTRAY
MR. PRESIDENT

1.

He is alone in the hall
red cup in hand
feather hat on head.

Outside the window, scattered corpses
knocked-down trees
and a handful of rabid dogs
roving about.

2.

He leans against
the empty space,
eyelashes glued to the glass,
toothless mouth chewing muttered words
about a vanished glory.

At a distance sit the royal guards
around a table,
barking at each other.

3.

Swollen
like a rotting apple,
he oozes black snakes
and false secrets.

4.

As he dozes,
he builds, in his daydreams,
a wailing country
with his stumbling speeches.

5.

Filled with pride, he stands
on the edge of the world
holding the bell of the final alarm, ready
to ride back to the beginning of creation
waving two torches,
one of God and one of battle.

6.

The President has no citizens
to profit from his great skill
as an artist.
The citizens have no President
to shape their thinking
with his endless tales
about killing monsters
raging like the sea.

7.

Biting his fingernails
with his bleeding gums,
he mourns his picture, fallen from the wall.

SOHEIL NAJM
translated by Haider Al-Kabi

"his picture": *Saddam's picture was everywhere. Iraqis used to say*
that the population of Iraq was 34 million: 17 million Iraqis and 17
million Saddams.

THE EXECUTION OF AN EXECUTIONER

for Sergon Boulus

O poet
He did not listen to your words
So he did not return to his village
And we did not remove him from his job.

He did not return and did not go away.
He was not expelled and he did not listen.

And so we chattered empty phrases
While the language died within us.

You, who had escaped from their cages,
They have dethroned you like lightning
And in the blink of an eye they dragged you
Out of the rat's hole.

They put you in another cage
With words that were sharp enough
To cut off heads.

And now, on the screen
The eyes watch you:
Eyes of the executed ones,
The missing ones,
The prisoners, the poor,
The handicapped,
The exiled and expelled.

On the screen
The eyes watch you:
The eye of an ear you cut,
The eye of a hand,

The eye of a foot,
And the eye of a chopped-off tongue.
The eyes of the country watch you
And dream of your execution—
Dream of the sweetness of your departing
And never returning, headsman.

When you are gone,
Life will return
To the poet's language.

O poet,
Write your poems now,
Now that he's in the pit
And rats wheeze in his ears,

Now, as the life returns
To the poet's language.

HANADI AL-NASSAR

translated by Sadek Mohammed

TOMORROW THE WAR WILL HAVE A PICNIC

Tomorrow the war will have a picnic:
Decorate the hospitals with medicines, bandages
And sharp lancets.

Tomorrow the war will have a picnic:
Dust off the graves
And dig fresh ones—
War detests the smell of rotting corpses.

Wash up with mud, then
Brush your teeth white so they'll gleam
In the darkness of its pompous entourage.

Throw fragile joys out of your heart—
War has no use for bubbles or balloons.

Tomorrow the war will have a picnic:
Prepare your bodies for pain,
Your limbs for amputation.
War's affection is heavy-handed—
It loves to mess with your body.

Tomorrow the war will have a picnic:
Abandon delicacy
And laughter.
War does not like chocolates
Or kissing in public—
These things are not good for the heart
Of the war
Which is having a picnic tomorrow.

Empty the salty streams
From the faucets of your eyes.
The war's blood pressure is high,
Its arteries hard,
So it doesn't like salt in its food,
Or on your cheeks.

Tomorrow the war will have a picnic:
Break mothers' hearts now,
So the force of their tears won't expand,
Cracking the crust of the earth,
Nor sleeping volcanos erupt
Inside our chests.

Tomorrow the war will have a picnic:
Turn off the moon hanging over the roof
So it won't dim the tracers and flares
That light up war's path.
Let death come in beauty and comfort, soft
As a pillow of angel's feathers.

Tomorrow the war will have a picnic:
Let's close the parks,
The gardens,
The flowered balconies,
To allow it to stroll at its ease.

Sweep those big, messy clouds from the sky
So they won't get airplane wings all wet
And swerve them from precise, pinpointed targets.

Tomorrow the war will have a picnic:
Plant flowers,
For graveyards will grow.
And besides, they will cheer up the dead
Who will hang in garlands from our necks,
Awaiting the Judgment Day.

Tomorrow the war will have a picnic:
Store water, bread, and air.
Because the war gets hungry now and then,
And if our tender bodies aren't enough to satisfy it—
Our childish pranks, our innocence, our dreams—
It will be compelled to eat the buildings,
Bodies sleeping in graves,
Books, streets and biscuits.
It will be forced to eat unshakable mountains,
Statues and stones—
Anything to feed its body of smoke,
Bullets and shrapnel.

Tomorrow the war will have a picnic:
We must go out to meet it—
Out of our bedrooms, our
Schools, barbershops, public libraries,
Mosques, shelters, *One Thousand Nights and a Night,*
Caves, post cards, fields, graves, trenches,
Bread bags, soft drink bottles,
Al-Tawhidi's *Isharat,* tooth brushes,
Ibn Malik's *Alfiyah, Rawdhat Aljinan,* family trees,
Cradles and news bulletins.

We have to come out from our
Skins and our milk names to meet it,
And join its parade
To the Al-Sallam graveyard.

Tomorrow the war will have a picnic:
Abandon delicacy,
Laughter,
Dancing,
Childhood,
Women,
Beds,
Cups of tea and milk,
Classroom desks,
And what's left of dreams
Splintered in corners.
No more chocolate,
No more kissing in public—
Things like these
Are not good for the health of the war,
Which is having a picnic tomorrow.

ABDUL RAZAQ AL-RUBAIEE
translated by Sadek Mohammed

GOD'S MONEY

from *Slightly Quarrelsome Texts*

On Al-Hamra'a street
The religious man passes with his prayer beads
The pauper passes with his barefoot dreams
The politician passes, full of schemes
The intellectual passes, lost in thought
Everyone passes in a rush, and pays no mind
To the beggar on the sidewalk, poor and blind
Only the rain is dropping in his palm
To God outstretched

ADNAN AL-SAYEGH

translated by Soheil Najm

A DROP

Absent-mindedly, night forgot
      A drop of water on your neck.
Absent-mindedly, I forgot
      My soul within it.

Now you're gone.
Ah, God—
If, absent-mindedly,
      Your hands should stroke
      That magic drop
You'll see me
      Like a genie
      Appear between them.

Reem Qais Kubba
translated by Soheil Najm

FROM HER BOOK, ONE MORE TIME

When
Her seesaw is me and she is my seesaw
When
Her two doves are shivering in my fingers
And her cup is full of my wine
When
Her space is redolent of my kiss
And her kiss is swimming in my space
When
The organ pipes shudder and the violins get drunk
When
Golden deer fly through the sky
And the skin of the earth starts to tremble—
The pearl of weeping becomes a river of firebrands!
That's how astonishment always comes out of her book....

AHMED ASHEIKH

translated by Soheil Najm

ILLUSORY VILLAGE

O lovely light
Passing away this night of love
You, enthralled by the stories in your blood:
By what the land said to the grass,
What the mountain said to the plains.
O lovely light
A flower is putting a crown on its head,
Conquering my kingdom and the laws of my soul,
And spilling me out in its hands.
I am a drop.
Do you see me?

What would you know of a star
That was not in any sky?
And what would you know of the power of a dream
Were you not, yourself, a dreamer?
What would you know about the masters of wheat
And the pride of the man in shackles,
The rough mountain women,
The blood that opens the wound,
Two hands spread to the wind,
Or a horse
Without a rider
Running free on the mountain?
And what would you know of the whims of the mind
Or about harvest nights?
And what would you know about the body of a woman
That wears its nudity
In the night when the cannons thunder?

In that place, each house is like a village.
The soul's village opens its windows to see

How houses look in the dark of night
How a star falls
How a cloud is torn by the wind
How fields look like medals on the shoulders of the land
How a women reaches orgasm
Or how the rain slaps me in the frosty nights.
There, hearths are brimful with fire.
A woman in love wears her slumber
Gets up warm in the morning
While another body of hers remains in bed
Pores oozing sweat and wine and lazy sleep.
Wait awhile!
You have gone back to love again
To die upon the altar of a woman
Glowing naked
And dying of love every night.

O lovely light
You will dream that you call up the wind,
That you grant the sea whitecaps and waves,
Make a mouth for the morning from kisses.
You will dream you build temples,
Toll the bells of an ancient tower
To announce the dance of the sea,
The wine of Easter,
The staircase to glory.

O you!
Who led us to be so alike?
Who told us to follow the footsteps of water,
To disappear in the wind,
To climb on the rocks,

Draw love on the sands,
Lie upon each other's beaches?
Only the wine knew the way
To make us magicians.

KHALIL AL-ASADI

translated by Sadek Mohammed

WHAT AN IDIOT

What an idiot I was
To think my heart was made of steel.
Little did I know
Your heart would magnetize it—
Suddenly, it was a beggar
In the presence of the Sultan,
Shaking like the tear of a bereaved mother.
Even though you set my eyelashes
On fire
Still I keep sowing my soul
And never once gathering fruit.

JALAL ZANGABADI
translated by Soheil Najm

THE UNSHOD LADIES WENT ON FOOT

The unshod ladies went on foot
To visit gold
Completely naked, but for the clink of anklets
And the scent of henna
Their mood was like an open window
And their hearts were captive
To the sound of the cicadas, hidden in heavy clouds
The flower was naked too
Except for its fragrance, floating in the air
The unshod ladies gathered
In a mirror
That was suddenly smashed—
And the sparrow, the female sparrow
Was perching nearby, singing for the wreckage

SHAKER LAIBI
translated by Sadek Mohammed

SCORPIONS ARE RELAXING IN THE DARKNESS OF THE GARDEN

Scorpions are relaxing in the darkness of the garden.
A little light upsets them.
Just like the truth—
A little logic
Changes its dimensions.
The scent of the dust they breathe
Grows old beneath their feet,
As myths grow old
Between your tender fingers
Stretching through the thickness of my hair.
Your fingers are frittering down my back
As if they were five lizards, petrified
Since time's beginning.
Are you still wet and waiting
At the doorstep?

SHAKER LAIBI

translated by Sadek Mohammed

BRINE ON THE WINGS OF SEAGULLS

When the poor negroes lost their first battle,
the sailors robbed me of my beloved's keepsake
And washed the smell of the ocean from my body.
Suddenly, I was a stranger to the sea,
the sea a stranger to me.
The water closed its eyes and bowed its head,
No more a refuge for the cast-out mariner.
On the front of my shirt
I wrote my beloved all that had happened,
and all that was still to happen:
I wrote: "Beloved, stretch out your hands
like shores of oleander."
I laid my shirt on the water
and, stirred by the hoped-for dawn,
I called on the seagulls
to carry my shirt to my beloved.
But the seagulls passed me by,
bearing nothing but the sea brine to the desert.

The water cast back my white shirt, its sleeves tied together.
Who then takes the mariner's shirt to the beloved?
Who, on this open sea, can show a cast-out mariner the path to land?
Who carries the body of this murdered mariner to Basra?
Who?
No one but the sea.

The sea looked strange; its shores were still.
Basra's negroes, soaked in brine,
pulled the Indian ships up to the merchants' doors.
Al-Sahib had not sent his seagulls as a sign of freedom.
Al-Sahib was sentenced to death
for rousing the poor negroes against the merchants.
Tonight, not Basra's palm trees nor the negroes' prayers

will hide him from the spies, the swinging lanterns in the soldiers' hands.
Tonight, beloved,
Nothing will shield Al-Sahib
Against the whips.
No one will rescue the lover
From the torments of his love.

Beloved. . . .

But love had died inside the mariner.
All the lovely women had boarded ships, eloped with sailors.
And the negroes were shivering sparrows, seized by ravenous cats.

Al-Sahib was hanged with a rope of merchants' shirts.

Beloved,
If you were there, would you cry,
or rejoice at the death of this infatuated lover?

When the poor negroes launched their second battle
I called on my beloved.
Their plight gave me an angry voice,
a voice discretion could not silence.

Beloved, as you swing here and there,
you split my suffering soul,
you rock my heart, like a naked lantern glowing in the rain.

Beloved, you must either give
your allegiance to the poor negroes or to the merchants.

Tonight, as I passed by,
I overheard some seamen talking,

pointing at me, their fingers gilded with tobacco:
"Last night, the sailors murdered that mariner.
That mariner—"
"Hush, lest he hear you—"
"has a beloved the Basra merchants will slay tonight."
Tonight I will take refuge in myself,
not for fear some spy will follow me and count my steps, and write:
"He passed by a negro, they shook hands,
      a turtledove hid between their palms,"
but to see you,
for my flesh is swept by your love.

And I saw you, let me confess that I saw you
like a lantern glowing in Basra's night.
I saw the seagulls flying, laden with letters from lovers to loved ones,
and coming back, laden with letters from loved ones to lovers.
Going and coming, and going and coming again,
wings no longer weighted down with brine,
going and coming between the sea and the harbor.
And I saw Al-Sahib, wrapped in water and wild grass,
going out in the evening, attended by Basra's lovers,
      and the negroes, and those
from distant cities, and Basra's negro singer, Tuman, enchanted
      with a thousand loves,
all going to a picnic on the beach of Al-Ashar, on boats
      all filled with oleander.

ABD AL-HASSAN AL-SHATHR
translated by Haider Al-Kabi

"Al-Sahib": *Though an Arab himself, Al-Sahib led a revolt by
African slaves against their Arab masters. The poet, Al-Shathr,
"disappeared" during Saddam Hussein's regime, making this
ode to freedom all the more poignant.*

A WHITE WINDOW

Since you are the apple of light
Beyond the clouds
I agreed to be its shadow
Under the trees stretching over
The horizon of absence.
And because you are the honey gold
Flowing between my hands
I agreed to be
The bees that floated
In the forest of light.
I searched for you
On roads through the wilderness
Till I became
The only path to you.
I am waiting for your horses
To stampede my heart
To cover my face
With the light of their dust.
I am waiting for my blood
To drink your clouds
So that my heart can see your radiance
And my mirror embrace
Your white sun
That rears on the back of the sky
While horses fly
Washing the day
With your light.
Because you are the sister
Of the sun
I became the brother
Of the darkness. . . .

I'll never return from this journey
On the long road to you,
Loosing my horse
To lead me to the sun.
I who am madly in love with you
And the thunder of your horses
Wait for your dazzling face
To emerge from the fogs of dawn.
You are the sun in the heart,
Your presence
A white window
Set against the blackness of the country. . . .

Every day I traveled long
Beside the shore.
The seagulls called to me
The women in love called to me
You called to me,
The lonely wanderer,
And you became my love.
Now I am like an axis—
Everything about me spins,
Spins, spins.

ZAIEEM AL-NASSAR
translated by Soheil Najm

THE SPINDLE

In her hand the wind quivers.
How often she sat near the door of the courtyard
To spin her childhood's days on the doorsteps,
Among the neighborhood women!
How she would pass the time
Dreaming her life spun into a thread
That stretched out beyond the horizon.
Her face covered with village freckles,
Eyes shadowed with kohl,
With her wild adornments,
Her *dayram* and *mestak* and tooth stick!
How much she misses those threads
And the fine wool amassed in her lap!
Now my hand holds her thread at one end—
And the spindle continues to spin!

HASHEM SHAFEEQ

translated by Sadek Mohammed

"Dayram": *bright red lip coloring*
"Mestak": *a bitter chewing gum*

THE NEEDLE

She sat and darned a sock, a skirt,
the threadbare curtains.
She drank her coffee in the shadows
then stepped outside
to examine the hem of her homeland.
She saw the vast desert
being torn like a dress.
Undaunted, she twirled
her needle till it twinkled,
then set off to sew up the tears
they had made in her country.

HASHEM SHAFEEQ

translated by Sadek Mohammed

WE ARE NOT DEAD

for Kadhim Kaitan

To no avail the doves cooing—
Our delights are cellars
And our time is ash.
We go, every sunset, to the river
Carrying the coffins of our days
Polishing our teardrops
And shrouding our fears.

We are not dead.
We still have the tearful embrace
Of sacrifice.
We compose our features,
Bandage our calendars,
Our disappointments,
And,
Under a spider's tent,
We still have the right
To conquer the city with kisses.

We return to our hospitals
Lighting lamps of regret
And reciting our elegies.
Our lifetimes are paper boats
Pushed to the waves by the hand of a trifling child
Where, fold after fold,
The sea takes our dreams
And wraps them in weeping.
Our lifetimes are withered leaves
That launched an attack on the sun
And fell in flames.
The fire now licks at our names,
Sewn together with splinters.

MUNTHIR ABDUL-HUR

translated by Sadek Mohammed

THAT IS MY LIFE

A stream of blood flowing
into a witch's mouth—
that is my life.

"Close the car door well.
If you fall in the middle of the road
no one will dare stop for you,"
said the woman sitting next to me
as I passed by the idols of fog
that raised their heads above the hills.

No one needs to listen anymore.
The flower of wisdom has been tossed
into a furnace of talk.
I keep chasing a mirage
like a magnetized arrow.
And I look back at my past
the way a child stares at the picture of his father
who was killed in the war.

They have all gone to the picnic.
The telegraph poles in the old streets
gather the noise of the drowsy gardens.
For some strange reason, people vanish
as soon as the need for them appears,
their steps like the tread of an executioner
approaching a head that drops into empty space.

The world has changed. Since when
has desolation been so hard and stubborn?
Who brought us such a huge amount of rust?
Which defeated general

has taught these restless hands the game of puppets?
Puppets in the vehicles,
on the shelves, in the streets, in the coffee shops,
puppets brandishing their axes against the flowers of the wind
—smuggler of roses and rain—
toothless puppets with heavily painted faces,
laughing in the face of the future,
singing by heart the songs of the hairy spiders.

Like fortunetellers
well versed in the ash business,
puppets hunting my future
with axes meant to knock down mountains.

What made the world so withered?

Drunk with the last fanfare of the day,
the men were murdered at night,
eyes filled with rain. . . .

A strange voice sings:
"Beware of this drunken youth—
he who has not spared himself
can cause you harm."

A spirit haunts the citadels of nothingness.
A gust of wind from an armored vehicle
coils around the neck of joy. . . .

What else?
You who stay up under the wing of night:
This which breaks free from God's sighs

is not a cloud—it is the thunderbolt
that brings down the keys of the unknown.

Words no longer suffice to console.
Bit by bit, a small white creature
will eat through all the passageways of earth
and a rumor will come from the battleships of night
about wolves who are dragging a three-headed shooting star.

Then the news will be confirmed at last—
that life was but a promise in the open air,
a death sentence on a beautiful morning,
a hope abducted by pirates,
an angel's mansion with broken windows,
a formula that failed
to bring consent and reconciliation.
A lover whose dreams
wear the seven shackles of impossibility—
that is my life.

ADAM HATEM

translated by Haider Al-Kabi

WHEN HE EXPLODED

1.

When he exploded
Nobody fell
Nobody fled
Nobody cared.
So he collected his fragments
And disappeared, ashamed.

2.

The wounds
Grew into enchanted trees.
Whenever the wind shook their branches
Unbelievable fruits fell down.

SALAM DAWAI

translated by Soheil Najm

THE SULTAN OF SORROWS

Every sorrow belongs to him.
He recounts them, sorrow by sorrow,
Then lights candles around them
And smiles.
So we crowned him the Sultan of Sorrows.

As for us
We have but one sole sorrow
Which we nurtured
Teardrop by teardrop.
We watered it
As mothers suckle their children.
So they called us slaves
And christened us
The slaves of the Sultan of Sorrows.

At last,
The Sultan whose slaves we are
Looked down and was amazed
At the beauty and nobility of our sole sorrow.
Jealous (for he had only common sorrows),
His Majesty issued an edict
Confiscating our sole sorrow.

Grave will be the days that we endure:
How can a wretched bunch like us,
Slaves of the Sultan of Sorrows,
Carry on our lives without our sorrow?
Bereft, we slaves began to chant a hymn:

"Oh bygone days,
The days of our sole sorrow,

How wonderful you were!
Why did you abandon us,
And leave behind
These boring days, days void of sorrow?
And you, O gracious Sultan
Why have you confiscated our sole sorrow?
Take pity on our children, if not us—
How can they grow up
Without a single sorrow?"

ABDUL-KHALIQ KEITAN

translated by Sadek Mohammed

A COUNTRY OUT OF WORK

Everybody here is out of work:
The workers in the factories and the officers in the offices,
All of them are out of work!
Those going early to the fields
And coming back tired at noon
Are also out of work.
The students and the teachers,
Whom the government pays handsomely
To master joblessness, are out of work.
The army and the police,
The children and the adults,
The women in the houses,
The imams in the mosques—all of them are
Out of work!
So long as there are strangers
Spreading darkness in our land,
Its children have no job but one—
The job of kindling sunrise from the ash
Of our extinguished sun.

ADIL ABDULLAH
translated by Soheil Najm

FLOUR BELOW ZERO

No sun in our plates
No shadows
No oil poured by the moon
No cloud we may stealthily
Milk from the sky.
Here is your share
Of ostrich feathers
And here is my share of cigarettes.
How much is left of the family's share?
Yesterday, flour ran out.
Before that, the sugar ran out.
No tea, no water, no air.
Eat the ration coupon then
And when you are full
Go out to the street.
Beware of the dolphins
And the whizzing ghosts!
Beware of insects!
Beware of the sun!
Take your full share of the street. . . .
What?
The street has run out!
Come back to your mothers' breasts then
Or to their wombs.
Take your share of darkness.
But the milk has run out.
Then go to the river,
Lie on your backs:
The moon will be a ball
Between your hands
And the sun will be a basket
And you . . .

Have you run out of your feathers?
And me . . .
Have I run out of cigarettes?
Our lives, have they run out?

Where have you put the girl?
I wonder
Whether we have run out of our little daughter.
Or perhaps they have stolen her?
Take this weapon
While I follow their steps.

They are hiding behind the door.
Their bellies are full.
Give them milk if you can.
These are our guests—
Leave the roof empty for them
So they can jump onto it.
Let every one of them take his share.
These are our thieves—
Give them shelter from the outdoors
And never,
Never slander them.
Pretend to be busy loading the gun. . . .
But the bullets ran out.
Occupy yourself then
By watching the stars
Or, go fetch water—
We'll knead these books
And newspapers to make bread.
Pick up the breadcrumbs from the ground,
Put them on the moon.

The moon has a silent light—
Engage it in conversation.

Everything may run out
Even nothing may run out—
We are in danger
And the world is a gun.
Thieves are in danger,
Bread is in danger.
Mothers have been stolen from their own tears.
Tell the children:
Sleep before the thieves come
And wake up after the bread comes.
Switch off the light and tell them
They have stolen the light from the lamp,
Just like they stole our old neighbor's ring.
And if they ask you about the ring,
Pretend to be busy combing your hair
Or
Busy yourself with a prayer. . . .

These are our children:
They have their share of lies
And a share of cake and bracelets
And swings.
They have wars to lose
And wars to win.
These are our children:
They ate their share of the storm
And were never sated.
Their inheritance is war,
Which they will also share. . . .

But you and I,
We will depart.
And when we finally run out of sacrifices,
You will demand your share of lamentation
And I
My share of curses. . . .

KAREEM SHUGAIDIL
translated by Sadek Mohammed

"roof": *Saddam's police would sometimes enter houses from their flat roofs.*

A WHEAT SEED

for Hasan, who is fond of dates

Papa
Papa
I want dates.
Take this date stone
Plant it on the roof of the house
Water it with your tears
Or
Leave it to the teardrops of the sky.
It will be a palm tree
With a long trunk
And fluttering fronds.
Stand in its shadow
Eat from its dates
And of its stripped fronds
Make a bag.
Do not draw a bird on the bag:
Your books may turn
Into airplanes.
If you draw a duck on the bag,
Beware of the river:
It may slip from your shoulder
And float all your things
In the water.
And if it gets stained from your paints,
Take a wave from the river and wear it.
Return to the palm tree:
Learn from the nightingale
How to read,
And from the palm fronds
How to withstand the wind,
And from the trunk
Learn thirst.

Make from its wood
A boat to save yourself.
Feed yourself by drawing
A fish.
Do not tell your friends about your colored shirt:
The river may dry out.
Do not tell them about the bag:
The palm tree may lose its clothes.
And about the boat
Do not tell them:
They may accuse you of lying.
If you wish, warble a song to them.
To the taste of dates,
Let them chant.
And if they see the palm tree
Tell them:
It's the neighbor's palm tree,
There are no dates in it,
No nightingales,
No doves.
It's a pretend palm tree—
Our neighbor washed it
And hung it out in the sun.
And if you need bread,
Take this:
A wheat seed. . . .

KAREEM SHUGAIDIL
translated by Sadek Mohammed

DRAWING

The teacher asked the students
To draw whatever they wanted.
The son of the principal drew
A new Chevrolet.
The son of the developer drew
A complex of markets and hotels.
The son of the party member drew
An armored car.
And the daughter of the school deliveryman
Drew a piece of bread.

LATEEF HELMET

translated by Soheil Najm

SHAPING

In the noisy restaurant's window
a little passer-by appeared,
his face all pale.
He was only there for two moments,
and dropped two beads of rain
on the cold, hard glass.
He thrust two hungry glances among the dishes,
and rubbed a small and dirty nose
on the chilly glass. The people's eyes
stared back at him, and he disappeared.
But the shape of his face
remained on the noisy restaurant's glass,
like a brand stamped on the fog.

MAHMUD AL-BRAIKAN

translated by Haider Al-Kabi

ELEGY FOR A COFFEE SHOP WAITER

In this vast and desolate place
Should I carry my table on my back?
Invite you to my home
And say: O guest,
Do you remember our two shadows in the sun
And our faces staring at the street,
Here in this vast and empty coffee shop?

Who shook the coffee shop's pine tree
Over the teacup?

O waiter!
I have encircled my table
With four walls
Lest I see you
Standing forever
Over my endless silence.

Nothing but the last day,
Then the funeral begins.
One minute,
And then you will be thronged by passers-by.
Watch out Ali!
The tea will be overturned from your hands.
Watch out Ali!

ABDUL-KAREEM KASID

translated by Sadek Mohammed

THE MIRROR OF THE EYE,
THE MIRROR OF MEMORY

This boy
At a time when sorrow burns in his blood
Crowned with childhood, charm and stones
Sits in secret, radiant
To count the embers of speech in his head
Turning words and longings loose
Like flocks of deer and wolves
In the forests of writing and paper.
This boy
Secretly opens a book, the mirror to a visionary eye.
This boy
Secretly reads a history
Of hidden memories, until he sees
A multitude of poets
Reading their long-lost poetry
In the resounding country of the void,
Accompanied by the quiet scritch of mice
And a thunderous silence. . . .

SAAD JASIM

translated by Sadek Mohammed

OF FREEDOM

A poet dies twice: once when he is published,
and once when a statue is erected to him.

—Mahmud Al-Braikan

You have invited me to explore
another continent with you,
but you wouldn't share the map.
I would rather sail
In my simple boat
And if we chance to meet,
That will be a meeting to remember.

You have offered me a house,
Decorated and comfortable,
In exchange for a song
That sticks to the instructions.
I would rather stay
On my horse's back
And roam
From wind to wind.

You have brought me another face,
Fresh and flawless, ideal in size.
Thank you, but
I don't feel like having a glass eye
Or a plastic mouth.
I don't want to wipe out differences.
I don't care for perfect symmetry.
Thank you, but
My distance is something I'd prefer to save.
Is the slave master not, at heart, a slave?

MAHMUD AL-BRAIKAN
translated by Haider Al-Kabi

AFFILIATIONS

On the everyday scene
I fix my gaze. But I have my dream,
My allegiance to the beautiful and far....

Against the daily clatter I nourish my milk-white voice
And clothe bare reality in the glow of thought.

I see all of history sketched in a single look.
I hear it—hear its secret pulse—in a single voice.
But these thoughts do not frighten me
Nor does death fascinate me.

And across the stations of grief,
Across hunger of soul and body,
Across light and shadow
I keep seeking eternity.

Alone and free, I belong in a thought
The dead wanted (but failed) to engrave on a stone.
I belong in the voice of primitive prophesies
In revolutions before their visions freeze
In heavenly love that the world refuses
In the lightning flash that reveals
              the face of the ages in a single blink of the eye
In the brilliant fields of beauty's flowering
In the childlike dream that fades but never dies
In the part of man that is lost in the dark
In that which sheds its light where meaning lies
In that which can't be owned, nor be defined.

MAHMUD AL-BRAIKAN
translated by Haider Al-Kabi

AN ATTEMPT AT MUSIC

1.

The music comes down, comes down
Like a bird, a bunch of grapes, a waterfall
And my heart flies with the bird
But my hand does not touch it.
The bunch of grapes touches my lips
But love has no knife to cut my emptiness.
And the waterfall comes and I become water to meet it,
But I collide with its boulders
And drown.

2.

Even the letters wear me out.
They alone visit me in my vast loneliness,
Without carrying in their hand a bouquet of sun,
Or a handful of moon
Or kisses of feathers.

3.

Everyone is dressed in someone else's clothes
Except me.
And when I found nothing to put on,
I went out naked . . .
Stark naked.

4.

The music comes down with sweet L's like children's lips,
Chirping R's, whispering S's
And dews of D's.

5.

The music comes
And I rise from death for it.
We meet like two orphans
Yearning for the feast of reunion.

6.

When I got acquainted with my blood
I found it besieged with birds.
And when I got acquainted with my heart
I found it brimming with alphabets.

7.

Happiness is a ballerina
And sadness is a Bedouin sitting on the ground
Playing on the *rebeck.*

8.

I liked my death
But when I tried to repeat it
I went insane!

9.

The music comes down, comes down
And the soul gets lost
Then vanishes.

10.

The music melts like silver
And sleeps like lovers worn out by long parting.
The music glitters and turns griefs into G's

And G's into gladness
That dances like a genie.

11.

What beauty!
The music plays on
And the letters sparkle.

12.

The rich man rejoices at the hotel's harem,
The singer at the nightclub's *dinars,*
The playboy at his new mistress.
But I am like music:
I only delight in what I find within,
And only make love with my letters.

13.

How long will the bleeding of letters torment me—
The protest of P's
The loss of L's in long-lost cities
The hypocrisy of H's
The betrayal of B's until death.
My God!
How long will the bleeding of letters torment me?

ADEEB KAMALUDIN

translated by Sadek Mohammed

AN ATTEMPT AT MAGIC

1.

On a midday in July
I sat under the sun's sharp tooth.
The heat crushed me until my clothes,
My heart, and my fingers were all wet
And two teardrops fell from my eyes,
Which, by the might of the Almighty, turned into two magicians.
Then two more teardrops fell
And the magicians became four
Who quietly circled around me.
Why are you crying? they asked in a timid voice.
I told them that the sun exhausted me,
And the sight of beauty sickened my heart.
I am destitute, the curse
Of hunger tortures me,
My loaf of bread is soaked in blood
And the Euphrates has burdened me with remorse.

The first one said: I am from India.
I can clothe you in golden attire.
The second said: I am from nowhere.
I can fly you from cloud to cloud.
The third one said: I am from Ad and Thamud.
It is I who can grant you the secret of pleasure.
The fourth one said: I am from China.
I can turn dreams to reality.
I said to them: hurry then, hurry up!
I have been buried by want
Just as an earthquake buries
An army of a thousand knights.

2.

The next day
I sat in my golden attire.
At my feet were a lovely little cloud,
A woman sweeter than honey,
And fingers that could make a dream
Come true.

3.

But when the sun rose to the middle of the sky
The golden threads melted,
My clothes turned to rags
And the beautiful cloud dissolved,
Making my feet look ugly.
The honey woman melted too,
And my lips tasted bitter like poison.
The dream fingers also disappeared
And my hands turned to skeleton bones.
Then I shouted: Oh my teardrops, Oh brothers, Oh friends
Where are you?
Where are your secrets and signs?

4.

The four magicians kept quiet,
But the fourth one took pity on my heart, which was broken
As a blind man's mirror.
He said: Do you want what's eternal,
And not that which passes away?
I answered: Yes.
He said: The only way
Is for you to touch one of our souls.
They nodded, and beckoned me closer.

The first of them stepped forth, stark naked
And said: We will,
Oh tortured soul! We will give you our letters.
Oh destitute one! We will teach you our signs.
But we fear that once you have learned them
You will scorn the world's gold and its golden attire,
You will despise the pride of nations,
You will be indifferent to a woman's legs and breasts,
You will deride all dreams.
And then, like us, you will be hollow,
Cold
Lost
And naked forever.

ADEEB KAMALUDIN

translated by Sadek Mohammed

AN ATTEMPT AT MADNESS

1.

The moon is at the door
Hung by its feet.

2.

Everyone became quiet
Like a broken string.

3.

Friends multiplied, here and there,
Like lies and nonsense.

4.

The meaning is imprisoned in itself.
No one can ransom it,
Even me.

5.

Those who died
Wrote their subversive poems.

6.

Yesterday I died
And in the morning, as usual, I woke up.

7.

Hunger is a letter.
All you need is to put it in an envelope
And send it to yourself—
Sorry—
To me.

8.

The woman died: the dream, the meaning and the dawn died too.
Her death was the occasion for forty disasters.

9.

Madness is beautiful
Because it is my full-of-birds post office box
And my full-of-darkness future.

10.

My letters protested
Against the mountains of grief which they bore,
So I repressed them with an iron fist
And patience and horror.

11.

The poet and the ruler died
The philosopher died
And the historian died.
But when the grocer died
Only then did the people protest.

12.

The only friend who survived
Sent me a letter full of serpents and owls.
It filled my house with horror.

13.

When I read my poems in a public
Celebration yesterday,
There was a huge crowd of people
I never dreamt of.

There were only my heart,
My table,
And my blood.

14.
Your love is a sign of light
And you, my love, are
A prophetess of darkness.

15.
When I wrote your name, I became confused.
I madly loved its letters.
I feared that people might behold them.
Rather, I feared that I myself would behold them.

16.
Where are you
To bring back the drums of Africa
The cock-and-bull stories of Asia
And the phantoms of the lower world to my blood?

17.
Your love has become a poem
Infatuating all the fools of the earth.
How wonderful!

18.
Your love led my poetry
To the essence of letters and signs
And led me to the ultimate—
Madness!

19.
Th . . .
The moon is at the door—
It has lifted one of its feet!

ADEEB KAMALUDIN
translated by Sadek Mohammed

CROAKING

I cannot stand exile anymore
And it cannot stand me.
I shall lose it like I have lost my homeland,
Palm tree
By palm tree.
Maybe I will lose myself as well.
When that happens,
I shall stand erect like a hungry crow
And paint the whole world with my croaking.

ABDUL-KAREEM KASID

translated by Sadek Mohammed

CREATION

Come close,
O neglected words,
And let me turn you
Into poems.

Ali Al-Imarah
translated by Sadek Mohammed

CALENDAR

Ever since we hung this calendar,
The wall
Has been oozing blood.
These days are a necklace,
Each one pierced through the middle.
How can you expect us to write
For coming generations?
How can we pour our memories
Into days that have
Holes in their hearts?

ALI AL-IMARAH
translated by Sadek Mohammed

UNARMED MORNING

Where do I get a falcon to rule the grandeur of the road
Or a hand to harvest the rabbits from the garden
Of the skull?
Even the lakes, so well-behaved in the morning
Dream about flying at noon.
I wonder, does Time wear a shirt dabbed with dusk,
Does it fall from autumn's pedestal on purpose,
Or do we merely heap up, cold, like a fallen soldier
In an ebony box . . . ?
Trachoma scars the vision of the heart,
Disrupting our connections,
As we trot between the whip and the reward
Toward a bastard splendor.
I wonder, who will save my grieving fingers
From the curse
Of the cocoon?
I wonder
Who will
Beckon . . . ?

SALMAN DAWOOD MOHAMMED
translated by Sadek Mohammed

MORE THAN ONE, LESS THAN TWO

Every line I write, I'm afraid,
will erase a line from your memory.

What negligent god has left you derelict?
What charm has made you write poems?
You look like a soldier from 1914.
How charming! How charming!
How can a poem be possible,
with so much shrapnel in your chest?
One splinter would burn up a volume of poems.
How can you extract poems and shrapnel from your chest
at the very same time?
Our fathers lied to us—
They never told us this was possible.

How have you aged and slackened in so little time?
God grant you a cheerful death!
You are the furious storm,
produced by words of peerless calm.

Has my silence worn you out? Has my forgetfulness frightened you?
Have you flung your hand out searching for me?
Have you hunted for something? Has something hunted for you?
Have you trusted that the gravedigger
will not put a cadaver in the grave,
but hay and lint and other trash?
A man is nothing but a nest.
"How the questions vanished,
leaving the answers alone!"
Have you found out who guides all these inhabited wagons,
and in what direction he is leading them?

There is no way, neither forward nor backward.
Who was it, before going to his garden, threw you here all alone
in this trash heap?

I'm afraid you'll say "you."
I'm afraid.

SABAH KHATTAB

translated by Haider Al-Kabi

NO WAY

No way
To the inn of the mists,
To the tavern of drunken joy. No way
To the girl who is waiting in al-Alqala'a
To tell you the way is clear.

No way.
There is no way for you,
No way for a bright guitar.
Only the spiders that are sucking
The light out of speech.
No way to the seashore,
Waiting for your star.
No way for the hope that is floating
In your blood.
You'll stay this way
Till the hidden statue falls.

No way to your way.
The eyes of half-humans
Are watching—
Did you know?
Let the wind be your eye.

So
You will build a village
Inside the cup of craziness
And see the strings of your guitar
Twanging on a moon
That rises from the depth of the Euphrates.

But a wind is rising,
Erasing the fog from the mirror,
Bearing with it the scent of hope.

Then the way will at last be clear
To the girl in al-Alqala'a,
To the tavern of joy,
To your awakening—
Until you, the guitar and the wind have gone deep
In the al-Alqala'a river
Forever.

ZAIEEM AL-NASSAR
translated by Soheil Najm

STRANGE AND LONELY CHILD SITTING IN A DARK GARDEN, THIS IS MY HEART

When I opened the book of the horizon
The light fell.
The heart was resounding a song
With bitter words.
I beheld, between me and the light
Walking corpses trying to
Kidnap my lightning and quench
My song.
Listening to the flute,
The soul slumbered.
The wounds were resounding:
Peace! Peace!
The windows were silent.
A wind lashed the heart—
A yellow storm blew,
Black water welled up
From the depths. The heart
Is my inkwell. I'll write
My sorrow on a soft blue cloud
To ease the pain.
My tree shakes its branches,
Awakens the birds to sing
The songs that the windows
Were waiting for,
Sinking
In the arms
Of darkness.
I'll pluck the mysterious
Rose
That sways in the soul:
The soul, a child
Strange and lonely,

Sitting in a dark garden.
Oh, fathomless soul
When will they plumb your depths?
Pure one,
Will they discover your whiteness,
Your spring full of
Endless green?
Quiet one,
When will the world be aware
Of your eloquent silence,
Flowering with pain,
Shivering fingers,
And the heart which never tires
Of its ink.
Houses of fog,
The morning,
The roses of the far fields,
The freezing waters,
And those who sleep on the sidewalk,
All waiting eagerly
For the sun.

RASMIAH MEHEIBIS ZAIR
translated by Soheil Najm

DOORS

from *Slightly Quarrelsome Texts*

I knock on a door
I open it
I don't see myself, but a door
Shaped like me
I open it
I enter
Nothing but another door
Oh, my God
How many doors between me and myself?

ADNAN AL-SAYEGH

translated by Soheil Najm

PERPLEXITY

from *Slightly Quarrelsome Texts*

My father said,
Share your vision with no one:
The road is mined with ears
And every ear
Is bound to another by a secret wire
That reaches right up to the Sultan.

ADNAN AL-SAYEGH
translated by Soheil Najm

IRAQ

from *Slightly Quarrelsome Texts*

Iraq that is going away
With every step its exiles take. . . .
Iraq that shivers
Whenever a shadow passes.
I see a gun's muzzle before me,
Or an abyss.
Iraq that we miss:
Half of its history, songs and perfume
And the other half is tyrants.

ADNAN AL-SAYEGH

translated by Soheil Najm

THE BLACK BOX

My wife's tears poured down; friends wrote me elegies; dust built up
on my bookcase and . . . and . . . and I did not care.

Worms ate their fill of my flesh, but did not leave, though overstuffed,
and I did not care.

It was pitch dark when God's angels, like phosphorus inside my grave,
wrote their report: "This virtuous worshiper of God, devoured by
worms, is a true believer," and I did not care.

God Almighty Himself visited me (I had decayed; my stench would
cause gold to rust) and He gently said: "I have read your poem
'Dolphins Swimming in God's Tears.'" He assured me that the
Judgment Day was soon to come, and I did not care.

Some creatures came, and, with great caution, lifted my skeleton and
placed it in a UFO, and I did not care.

Their skillful, all-powerful devices revived my crumbling bones, and I
did not care.

The wise devices saw their mistake, and cured me of—not caring!
Then my questions poured out about everything, from the tears of
my wife to the Judgment Day.

I looked at a screen in front of me: the answer was blinking there.
"Dear earthly friend: About the past—it's better *not* to care."

Jamal Mustafa

translated by Haider Al-Kabi

THE TRANSIENT THINGS

Have a talk with Time.
Try to understand him,
and let him understand you.
Reconcile yourself with him—
forget the conflicts,
the repeated offenses,
his axe's strokes.
Go out together for a picnic:
go to his museum and have a look
at the wonders there.
Be patient, please: there's more
to this museum than history.
Time may open up
his treasure chest, show you
his glittering jewels.

Yes, the museum harbors
instruments of war. But look,
there's more: sculpture, pictures
of Venus, garden walks.
Give Time a chance.
Not every tree in his garden
conceals a crime.

Take off the dark glasses:
look at the river, not
at the fighting ships.
Sit up straight; show a little
respect when you sit with Time.
It's more than just a museum, it's
the life all around you, the air
of the green fields and farms,

filled with the sound and sparkle
of birdsong and butterflies.

Don't look on Time as your enemy.
Enough of war!
Regard it as being no more
than another museum exhibit.
Whether you choose to go inside
or stay away,
look upon these modern ruins
as though they, too, were ancient monuments.
Try to walk by without harm.

And when you're tired of this museum,
freedom can be found
in death. Or, why not
make a world that's all your own,
teeming with creatures who are proud
that they belong to you? A world
outside this world. How can you
discover such a world?

Look! Simply look—
Look at the beauty around you.
Take a small vial of perfume
from the earth.
Look at the things that are gleaming
in your hand—the dust and the grain,
the things that are dear to your heart.

Take this path to happiness,
and leave the myths behind.

Don't knock at the doors of kings.
Walk on, walk on without regret
for what you leave behind.
Let your footsteps be your country
and celebrate the road
as each path hands you onward to the next.

Delighted, be always delighted.
Be fruitful like any tree
beside a river.
Take your delight
from the earth—
where else will you find it?
Go with an elegant grace
even in the midst of ruins,
and let the world be yours
without its sad mythologies,
its labyrinths.

Don't carry weapons.
Don't pile up treasure,
or seek a grand title.
Don't engrave your image
on a kingdom's coins,
or sign your name
to secret documents.

Don't be a statue
in a public square.
Don't build a museum
or be a museum exhibit.
As you walk this earth,

don't act like a priceless antique,
don't mask your face with mosaics.
Don't play the buffoon
or the martyr.

Put your exile
on the tip of your tongue,
and say a kind word with a smile,
without a trace of arrogance or grandeur.
Kind words have neither arrogance nor grandeur.

The house of your love
Is the nightingale's tear drops.

Be sure to tell him:
I love you
From the heart of my heart.
From the heart of my heart
I love you.

The house of your love
Is the nightingale's wings.

RA'AD ABDULQADIR
translated by Soheil Najm

MY BROTHER'S WAR

Get up, brother; the war is over.
They have taken your tank to the smelter
But your rifle still lies on the mountain.
At last, the sand has erased your courage
And farmers plant fields where you fell.
The trees that you planted
Have died. The enemy has taken the mountain
You vowed you would never abandon.
From its ice-covered summit
They lowered your banner, which always stood firm
Till your downfall.
They've plundered your uniform and your splendor
And no matter how dead,
They kept crumpling your corpse with their bullets.
Even with worms coming out of your eyes,
Your big heart, they couldn't
Believe you were dead—
You had been their worst nightmare.
Get up, brother; the war is over.
The children have surrounded the garden.
The balls of fire and metal
Have cooled, and the children
Now kick them around—
Except for the ball that fell next to you
And tore you apart from your body.
We're back in the village now,
Without war and without enemies.
Horizons of dewy nightingales
Surround our pillows.
Slowly, we're forgetting our old wounds,
And though our daggers bring back memories,
All we really want

Is that our dogs not bark for anyone
Except our guests.
My mother is still in bed.
I spoke with her of your height and your strong arm
And it delighted her
That they couldn't find shoes that would fit you.
She asked me
How you were sleeping
And it saddened me to tell her
That you hadn't slept for seven years,
That a shell from a huge strong cannon
Crushed your ribs
And stripped you of your youth.
So I let the sun set
Upon your names and dreams,
Let lie at rest the scattered dust
You have become.
Between your life, your death, there lies
A distance of six children.

TALEB ABD AL-AZIZ

translated by Haider Al-Kabi

THE HANGING GARDENS OF DEATH

Baghdad, August 2004

It is your country, oh fool,
Even if its land is too narrow for a rose.
It is your country, oh enchanted one,
Even when it's hard to find a song to comfort you.
Oh lonely passer-by,
It is your country, you who are wounded by hope.
It is your country, your sad sonata, your country
Even when clouds of turbans closed its horizon. Your country
Even when the swords of veiled men closed its windows,
Even when its routes were mined with bombs.
It is your country, your melancholy song and the graves of your dear ones.
Your country, where the song of the desperate
Is your only weapon. Your country
Even when the chariots of its dreams
Were broken in the burning daybreak.
It is your country, its roses your roses
Even when it turned its Babylon
Into Hanging Gardens of death.

It is your beloved and your country, even when
It kneaded the clay of its dawn with the blood of holy men
And the tears of chaste women.
This is the widows' republic, land of your soul held captive,
And then the republic of fear.
Your country, a daffodil in Karkh
Befriending the dew of daybreak prayer.
Your country, even when its sweetest hearts
Are in the graveyards.
It is your country or your torment,
Your country or your despair,
Your country or the ashes of your hopes—there is no difference.
It is your country and your intimate lover,

Your dream's companion and the river of your grief.
It is your country: you, tormented and expelled.
Your country, you who take refuge in exile
From the hot sands of its valley.
It is your country and the wood fire of memory
In your soul's forest, your country
Even when the wings of its doves were broken,
Even when the angels left its holy cities.
It is your country even when its thorns
Crowd the roses of your heart,
Your country even when its shrapnel pierced
The body of Mary in her churches.
It is your country and the princess of your heart,
Then it is the night that fell on Baghdad,
And still it is your country, even when the train of its days
Has stopped at lost stations, its rails turned to rust.

It is your country, oh loser in the garden of evil winners.
And still, it is sonata roses and the cooing of doves:
Your country is the hope on her lips
Like the sun on a chilly day.
It is your country singing its own requiem,
Your country when even its victories
Felt cold as defeat.
It is your country and the nun of hope in your broken cities,
Your country, a candle
Besieged with barbed wire.
It is your country, even when happiness was outlawed.
And still, it is the princess of your heart:
Your sonata, even when your life
Was a hollow drum in an empty city.

It is the tenderness that penetrates when you have lost
The way back to your homeland,
The sweetness of Baghdad's jasmine and the sadness
Of its river banks.
It is your country and the burning of your home. Your country
Even when its hopes are desert wastes, like the passage
From Heet to Arar.
It is the country you grieved, the grindstone of your fear
And all your losses.
The country that weighed you with longing, despair, yearning and love,
Your country, where the honey of tomorrow ripens
In the bitterness of today,
Where your insides sing out your sonata.
Your country of secret gardens,
Where hope grows in hiding, like a black lily.
Your country is rising from the ashes of your heart—
It is your country, oh fool, the princess of your dreams and your sonata,
Last song left standing in Baghdad,
Tender and filled with love.
The sails of its tomorrow are ripped and torn, but... it is smiling.

ALI ABDULAMEER
translated by Soheil Najm

ASSUMPTIONS

for Galina

We shall assume that
When you come,
You will come snow-white
From the cortex of our days
Anointing our heads with water
And granting our times more tenderness.

We shall assume that
The wind will unbutton its dress
And rub its smooth skin
With rose water
And ambergris
Spilling the scent of the breeze
Upon our dark complexions.

We shall assume that those who have returned
Will sift bygone times
So that only the permanent,
That which heals the pangs
Of love and war,
Remains.

We shall assume that when we
Tell the sea
That its breasts
Are not good for
Flirtation
Or suckling,
It will suggest a truce
With our old boats.

We shall assume—just an assumption—
That we will sleep on the roofs of our houses
To cool the summer's heat,
That we will wake to summer mornings
Aromatic with our mothers' bread.

We shall assume that we will see our fathers
Grow old before our eyes
And that our sons will master their languages
And we will say "farewell!"
To all our loved ones
         when they die.

We shall assume that we will fall in love with women
As bashful as our neighbors
Or stroll at ease through unknown neighborhoods
Or get drunk in Baghdad's or Basra's taverns
Or light a candle in a church near Babul Muadham
Or pass through the Gate of Wishes at the Imam's shrine
So that the sky will sprinkle us with butterflies
That sparkle like the mirrors of his tomb.

Or we will mourn without fear
With those who mourn Hussein
To purify our souls
To reopen the roads
And bridge the gaps.

We shall assume that we will
Rename all things
To encourage the believers in the sun,

And women will change their night-black clothes
For bright ones.

We shall assume that we will
Witness a rosy Euphrates sunrise
That changes the balance of
Light and darkness.

We shall assume that you will come.

We shall assume that . . . .

Please, don't let us . . . . like idiots.

Come!

Amen.

SADEK MOHAMMED
translated by the author

"We shall assume that . . . .": *The long ellipses in the two*
lines above represent the "technique of silence" in Arabic poetry.
Readers are asked to participate in the creation of the poem by
filling the blanks with their own thoughts and feelings.

OH HUMANITY

Oh humanity
I am your grateful son.
Every man my father's age
Is my father.
Every woman my mother's age
Is my mother.
All these little ones
Are my children,
And this dog
Who sits beside me
Is my friend.
Oh humanity
Oh my family
I am your grateful son.

ALI AL-BAZAZ
translated by Soheil Najm

Notes on the Contributors

Book titles are translated from Arabic.

ALI ABDULAMEER was born in Babel in 1955. He is author of *Two Hands Referring to the Idea of Pain* (Baghdad, 1993), *Take the Songs as a Praise for Your Absence* (Beirut, 1996), and *Chapters in Contemporary Music.*

ADIL ABDULLAH was born in Baghdad in 1955. He is author of *The Museum of Nothingness* (Baghdad).

RA'AD ABDULQADIR was born in 1953 and died in 2003. He is author of *Let the Nightingale Wonder* (Baghdad, 1996) and *A Hawk, a Sun Over His Head* (Baghdad, 2002).

KHALIL AL-ASADI was born in Baghdad in 1950. He is author of *Primitive Hymns* (Baghdad, 1978), *The Pipe of the Time* (Baghdad, 2000), and *Your Perfume Remains in the Place* (Baghdad, 2005).

AHMED ASHEIKH was born in Najaf in 1970. He is author of *The Bird of Now* (Baghdad, 2000).

TALEB ABD AL-AZIZ was born in Basra in 1952. He is author of *History of Grief* (Baghdad, 1994) and *What the Lamp Cannot Reveal* (Damascus).

ALI AL-BAZAZ was born in Nasiria in 1958. He is author of *A Candle Only Hides the Sun* (Holland) and *The Waiter of My Dreams* (Holland).

MAHMUD AL-BRAIKAN was born in Basra in 1931. Though known for refusing to publish his work, he was one of the pioneering Arab poets of the twentieth century. In 2002 he was murdered in his house, a crime that was never resolved.

SALAM DAWAI was born in Baghdad in 1970. He is author of *That Bitter Rain* (Baghdad, 1998).

ADAM HATEM (pen name of Saadun Hatem) was born in 1957 in the province of Maysan. He died in Lebanon in 1993. He is author of *No One* (published posthumously by Korras, Beirut, 1996).

LATEEF HELMET was born in Kirkuk in 1947. He is author of *Allah and Our Small City, The Braids of That Girl Are My Tent Summer and Winter,* and *The Good Word Is a Rose.*

MUNTHIR ABDUL-HUR was born in Basra in 1961. He is author of *Necklace of Mistakes* (Baghdad, 1992) and *Exercise in Oblivion* (Baghdad, 1997).

ALI AL-IMARAH was born in Basra in 1970. He is author of *Running After a Standing Thing* (Basra, 1998) and *Empty Places* (Basra, 1998).

SAAD JASIM was born in Babel in 1960. He is author of *Spaces of the Speech Child* (Baghdad, 1990).

HAIDER AL-KABI was born in Basra in 1954. He is author of *Bombardment* (Damascus, 1998).

ADEEB KAMALUDIN was born in Baghdad in 1953. He is author of *Details* (Baghdad, 1976), *Divan* (Baghdad, 1981), and *The News of the Meaning* (Baghdad, 1996).

ABDUL-KAREEM KASID was born in Basra in 1947. He is author of *The Bags* (Beirut, 1975), *Knocking at the Doors of Childhood,* and *Picnic of Pain.*

SABAH KHATTAB was born in Tikrit in 1956. He lost his literary manuscripts during journeys in exile across Iran, Afghanistan, Pakistan, and New Zealand. He eventually settled in Australia.

ABDUL-KHALIQ KEITAN was born in Misan in 1969. He is author of *Emigrants* (Beirut, 1998).

REEM QAIS KUBBA was born in Baghdad in 1967. She is author of *Seagulls Committing Flying* (Baghdad, 1991), *Celebrating Wasted Time* (Baghdad, 1999), and *I Close My Wings and Steal Time for Writing* (Cairo, 1999).

SHAKER LAIBI was born in Iraq in 1956. A writer, poet and painter, he is author of *Stone Fingers* (1976), *The Text of the Three Texts* (1982), *A Call for Help* (1984), *Rhetorics* (1988), *Metaphysics* (1996), *How?* (1997), and *The Sicilian Stone* (2001).

DUNYA MIKHAIL was awarded the United Nations Human Rights Award for Freedom of Writing in 2001. Her latest book is *The War Works Hard* (New Directions, 2005), which won the P.E.N. Translation Award. Her books in Arabic include *The Psalms of Absence*, *Diary of a Wave Outside the Sea*, and *Almost Music*.

SADEK MOHAMMED was born in 1964. He holds a Ph.D. in English Literature from Pune University in India. Currently he is Associate Professor of English at Al-Mustansiriyah University and serves as an editor of *Gilgamesh*, Iraq's cultural magazine in English.

SALMAN DAWOOD MOHAMMED was born in 1957. He is author of *Earthly Clouds* (1995) and *My Identifying Mark* (1996).

JAMAL MUSTAFA was born in Basra in 1958. He is author of *Unreasonable Rain on the Romantic Hunchback with his Flute Piercing the Breeze* and *The Black Box*.

SOHEIL NAJM was born in Baghdad in 1956. He is author of *Deflowering the Phrase* (Beirut, 1994) and *I Am Your Carpenter, Oh Light* (Damascus, 2002), and translator of *The Gospel According to Jesus Christ* by Jose Saramago and *The Serpent and the Lily* by Nikos Kazantzakis. Soheil is editor of *Gilgamesh*, Iraq's cultural magazine in English.

HANADI AL-NASSAR is an Iraqi woman poet born in Nasiria in 1975.

ZAIEEM AL-NASSAR was born in Nasiria, al-Alqala'a, in 1957.

ABDUL RAZAQ AL-RUBAIEE was born in Baghdad in 1961. He is author of *An Attachment to the Last Death* (Baghdad, 1986), *The Summary of Mistakes* (Geneva, 1999), and *Hanging Gardens* (Muscat, 2000).

ADNAN AL-SAYEGH was born in Najaf in 1958. He is author of *She Waits for Me at the Monument* and *The Man Who Stayed Awake in His Delirium*. He was awarded the Hellman-Hammet International Poetry Award in New York in 1996 and the International Poetry Award in Rotterdam in 1997.

HASHEM SHAFEEQ was born in Fallujah in 1955. He is author of *Familiar Poems* (Baghdad, 1978), *Household Moons* (Damascus, 1980), and *An Apparition from Pottery* (Beirut, 1991).

ABD AL-HASSAN AL-SHATHR was born in Basra in 1952. A graduate of the Teachers' Training Institution, Al-Shathr had published a few highly promising poems before his mysterious disappearance around 1981. He is believed to have been executed for his nonconformist political stance.

KAREEM SHUGAIDIL was born in Baghdad in 1956. He is author of *The Script of Pain* (Baghdad, 2005).

RASMIAH MEHEIBIS ZAIR is an Iraqi woman poet, born in 1955 in the province of Dhi Qar.

JALAL ZANGABADI was born in Zangabad, Diyala in 1952.